Contents

Any words appearing in bold, **like this**, are explained in the Glossary.

Was your pet once wild?

You may think that you just have a pet snake, but the snakes people keep as pets are very close to their wild relatives. Finding out more about the wild side of your pet snake will help you give it a better life.

Pet snakes are really the same as snakes in the wild. If you are lucky you may even have seen a wild snake.

There are many snakes that live in the wild as well as in captivity.

4

The Wild Side of Pet
Snakes

Jo Waters

www.raintreepublishers.co.uk
Visit our website to find out more information about **Raintree** books.

To order:
☎ Phone 44 (0) 1865 888112
▤ Send a fax to 44 (0) 1865 314091
▭ Visit the Raintree Bookshop at **www.raintreepublishers.co.uk** to browse our catalogue and order online.

First published in Great Britain by Raintree, Halley Court, Jordan Hill, Oxford OX2 8EJ, part of Harcourt Education.
Raintree is a registered trademark of Harcourt Education Ltd.

Editorial: Melanie Copland and Sarah Chappelow
Design: Richard Parker and Tinstar Design Ltd (www.tinstar.co.uk)
Illustrations: Jeff Edwards
Picture Research: Mica Brancic and Charlotte Lippmann
Production: Duncan Gilbert

Originated by Ambassador Litho Ltd
Printed and bound in China by South China Printing Company

10 digit ISBN 1 8444 3932 1 (hardback)
13 digit ISBN 978 1 8444 3932 4 (hardback)
09 08 07 06 05
10 9 8 7 6 5 4 3 2 1

10 digit ISBN 1 8444 3938 0 (paperback)
13 digit ISBN 978 1 8444 3938 6 (paperback)
10 09 08 07 06
10 9 8 7 6 5 4 3 2 1

British Library Cataloguing in Publication Data
Waters, Jo
The Wild Side of Pet Snakes
639.3'96
A full catalogue record for this book is available from the British Library.

Acknowledgements
The publishers would like to thank the following for permission to reproduce photographs: Ardea pp. **9** (Elizabeth Burgess), **24** (Ian Beames), **27**; Bruce Coleman p. **5** (NHPA/Daniel Heuclin); Digital Stock p. **21**; FLPA pp. **5, 10, 26**; Harcourt Education Ltd/Tudor Photography pp. **11, 13, 15, 17, 19, 22, 23, 25, 29**; NHPA pp. **4** (Karl Switak), **6** (Otto Pfister), **7** (Daniel Heuclin), **14** (Karl Switak), **16** (Karl Switak), **20** (Stephen Dalton), **28** (Daniel Heuclin).

Cover photograph of an emerald tree boa reproduced with permission of Corbis (Joe McDonald). Cover inset photograph of a common racer snake reproduced with permission of Corbis (Michael & Patricia Fogden).

The publishers would like to thank Michaela Miller for her assistance in the preparation of this book.

Every effort has been made to contact copyright holders of any material reproduced in this book. Any omissions will be rectified in subsequent printings if notice is given to the publishers.

A snake may not be a suitable pet for you. It needs special care and equipment. Snakes are not very friendly. They won't play with you or fetch a ball.

If you decide to have a snake, make sure you choose a suitable **species**. Some snakes can grow up to 6 metres (19 feet) long!

Pet pythons look just like their wild relatives.

Types of snake

There are over 3000 **species** of snake. There are small, shy snakes, like the grass snake, and large tree snakes, like the python. There are even sea snakes and water snakes.

Some snakes kill their **prey** by wrapping themselves round it and squeezing it until it stops breathing. These are called constrictor snakes. Others poison their prey by biting it and injecting poison called **venom**. These are called **venomous** snakes.

Venomous snakes are never suitable as pets and should only ever be kept by very experienced snake handlers.

A fully grown boa constrictor can reach 6 metres (19 feet)!

Pet snakes are the same as wild snakes. Snakes cannot be tamed like other pets and you should not handle them very much.

There are all sorts of **breeds** of snake. Corn snakes, king snakes, ball pythons, and garter snakes are kept as pets.

Different sizes

Snakes can be small or grow really huge. Even the smallest types of snake, like garter snakes or ball pythons, can grow to between 90 centimetres (35 inches) and 1.5 metres (5 feet).

Rattlers

Rattlesnakes got their name because they have a rattle in the end of their tail. They shake this to warn animals away.

Where are snakes from?

Snakes can be found all over the world. Pythons live across South-East Asia, and West and Central Africa. Boas can be found in North, Central and South America, Eastern Europe, Africa, and the Arabian Peninsula.

Sea snakes

*Sea snakes live in the Pacific and Indian oceans. They live in the **tropical** parts of the world, where the seas are warm.*

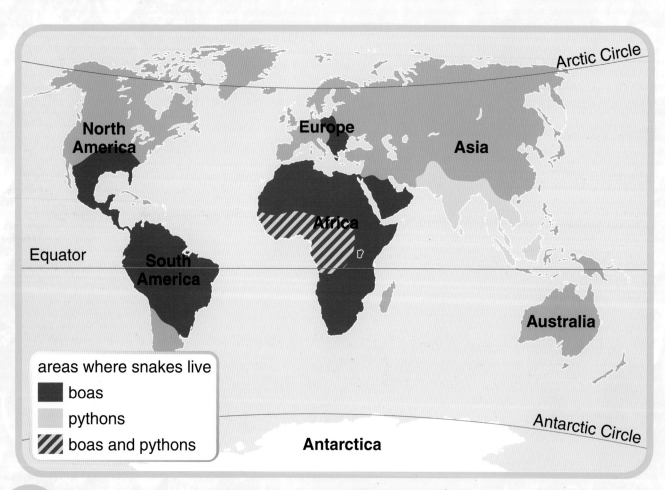

This map shows where wild snakes can be found.

Ask the breeder to show you how to pick up snakes.

Choosing your pet

If you decide to buy a snake, make sure you get it from a good **breeder**. Never buy animals that have been caught from the wild, as it is cruel.

When you choose your snake you should make sure it is healthy. It should have bright eyes and be active and alert. It should have a clean, firm body, smooth skin, and a clear mouth and nose. A snake should flick its tongue in and out when something is held in front of it.

9

Snake habitats

Wild snakes live in all sorts of **habitats**. Some, like the emerald and Amazon tree boas, live in **tropical** forests in tall trees. Others, like the Kenyan sand boa, live in dry areas like deserts. They hide under rocks or in the sand. Grass snakes live in meadows, grasslands, small woods, and by streams and lakes.

Snakes also live in the sea and in rivers and lakes. There are over 50 **species** of snakes that live in water.

The coral snake lives around coral reefs, rocky shores, and sometimes in salty swamps.

The best vivariums have a glass front so you can see the snake and light can get in.

Housing

Your snake's tank must give it all the things it would need in the wild. A snake tank is called a **vivarium**. The vivarium should be heated to the right temperature for your snake. Ask your vet for advice.

Tree snakes need a tall vivarium containing things to climb. Other snakes, like garter snakes, need a bowl of water to bathe in. All snakes need a nest box where they can hide and rest. Shredded paper is the best bedding.

Snake anatomy

Snakes are long, slender **reptiles** with no legs. Their skin is made up of **scales**.

Snakes never stop growing. They shed their skins to let themselves grow. This is called moulting. Young snakes grow more quickly than adults so they moult more.

Swimming

*Sea snakes have **adapted** to the water. They swim with a wriggling motion. They have a flattened tail that acts like a fin to paddle them through the water.*

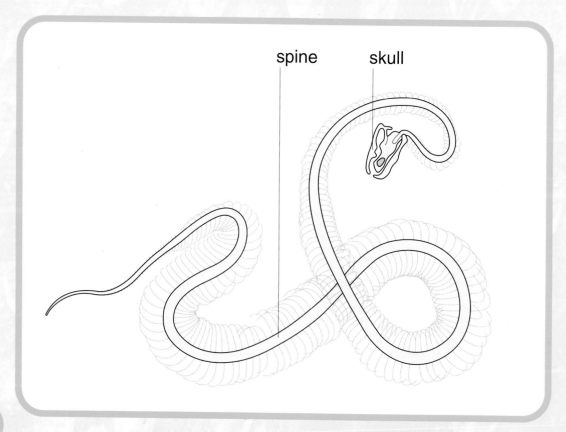

spine   skull

This drawing shows the skeleton of a snake.

Never pull off a snake's skin yourself. You could injure the snake. If there is any skin that doesn't come off properly, take your snake to the vet.

How to pick up a snake

Some snakes are very delicate and need careful handling. Pick up small snakes with two or three fingers held lightly around their middle.

Handling

Pet snakes have the same **anatomy** as wild snakes. Snakes do not feel slippery or cold. In fact they are warm and their skin is dry. Their scales sometimes feel slightly rough.

If you are picking up a bigger snake, use both hands, but don't squeeze too tightly.

13

Senses

Wild snakes have very sensitive senses, including taste and sight. But they also have some special senses.

Snakes don't hear like humans do. They don't have ears. They use their whole bodies to pick up the **vibrations** that make sounds. They use this sense to 'feel' where **prey** is.

Boas, pythons, and pit vipers can sense heat. They have special sensitive heat pits on their faces.

Snakes use the heat pits above their lips to sense the body heat of their prey.

Pet snakes use the same senses as their wild relatives.

A snake flicks its tongue out into the air and catches particles. It brings its tongue back into its mouth to taste the smell particles. This also can tell it about where it is and who is near it.

This snake is using its tongue to taste and smell.

Snakes don't have eyelids. Instead, they have a clear piece of skin over their eyes to protect them. They can't see very well, so rely more on their very sensitive hearing.

Movement

Snakes use their muscles to move their bodies. They use special **scales** on their bellies and sides to grip the surface they are moving on. Snakes like tree boas can climb very tall trees in this way. They also grip on with their tails and curl their bodies around branches.

Burrowing

Burrowing snakes usually have smooth scales that allow them to slide through the sand or soil easily. They have flattened noses that they use to shovel earth aside.

The sand boa has a special flat nose to help it burrow.

Sliding

Pet snakes move in the same way they would in the wild. Their muscles are very strong. They can coil around things to climb them. They use their belly scales to slide along the ground. Belly scales are usually large and rectangular to help the snake grip.

Your snake can climb as it would in the wild if you put branches in its tank.

Snakes are good at escaping! They can slither through very tiny gaps, so make sure that your tank has no holes in it.

What do snakes eat?

All snakes are **predators**. This means they eat other animals. Some eat worms and insects. Others eat small **mammals**, birds, and fish. Some, like the king cobra, eat other snakes.

The green anaconda can grow to be at least 10 metres (33 feet) long. It catches and eats large **reptiles** like alligators and turtles. The amethystine python from Australia can reach 8.5 metres (28 feet) long and will even eat wallabies.

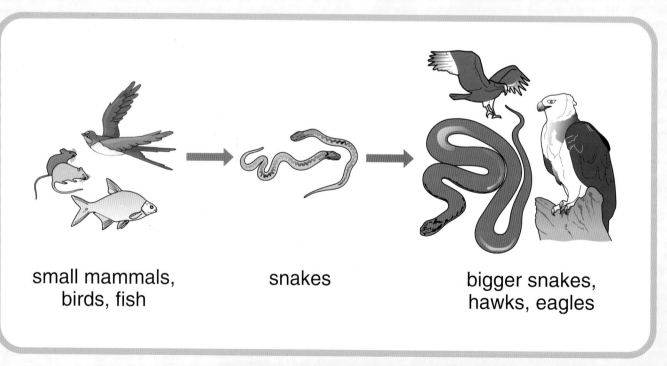

small mammals,   snakes   bigger snakes,
birds, fish   hawks, eagles

Snakes fit into a **food chain** like this.

Snakes do not need to eat very often.
They can eat a huge amount in one go.
An anaconda that has eaten an alligator
may not need to eat for many months.

Fussy eaters

Some snakes do not like dead food and will refuse to eat it. Others will go for long periods without eating. If you are worried, ask your vet.

Pet snakes need to eat similar food to wild
snakes. This will help to keep them healthy.
So you need to feed animals to your pet snake.

You can buy frozen mice and
chicks. You need to defrost
them before you feed
them to your snake.

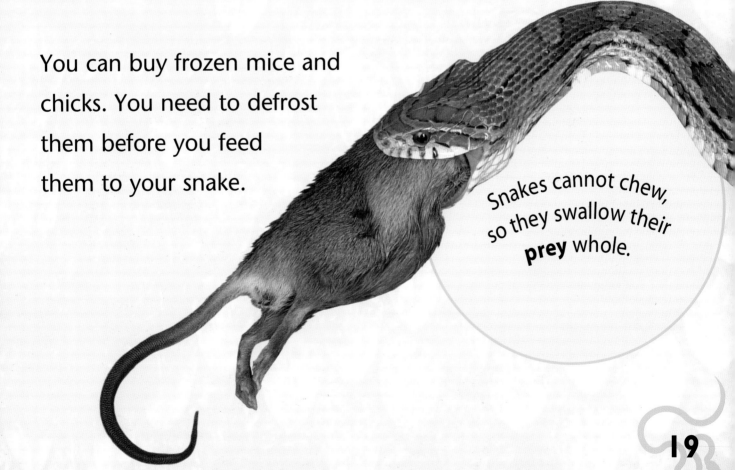

Snakes cannot chew, so they swallow their **prey** whole.

Hunting and playing

Snakes use different ways to hunt for their **prey**. Some snakes rely mostly on their senses of smell and hearing to find prey. Others use their heat pits to feel when animals are near. They do not use their poor eyesight very much.

Venomous snakes, like cobras or mambas, have fangs. These are special hollow teeth that inject **venom** into an animal. The spitting cobra can spit venom through the air for up to 2.5 metres (8 feet).

A striking snake rears up and bares its fangs.

Snakes will not move very much in **captivity.** This is because they don't need to hunt or avoid danger. Snakes do not play with each other. Even young snakes behave like adult snakes right from when they are born.

If snakes don't need food, they will curl up somewhere comfortable and rest.

Do snakes live in groups?

In the wild, snakes do not live in groups. They are not **sociable** animals. They usually only come together to **mate**.

Good mums
Female rattlesnakes will often stay with their babies for over a week. They leave their young after they have found food and know their way around.

Some pregnant female snakes will stay together in groups until their babies are born. This is for protection. Then the mother snakes and their babies all go their separate ways.

This female adder is protecting her young.

Just like wild snakes, pet snakes are not sociable animals. They will live with other snakes, but they do not need company. If you want your snake to live with another snake, first check with a vet or **breeder** to make sure they will not attack each other.

This snake is happy living on its own.

Snakes are not friendly pets and you cannot play with them. You should only handle them when you need to clean their cage or give them a health check. Too much handling can damage delicate snakes.

Sleeping

Wild snakes all need to sleep. They rest under rocks, in trees or in long grass or shrubs.

Snakes living in countries with hot summers and cold winters hibernate when the weather gets colder. This is a special type of sleep where the snake's body slows down and gets cooler. The snake doesn't wake up to eat or drink, and can hibernate for 6–8 weeks. If the weather is really cold, some snakes will hibernate for up to 4 months!

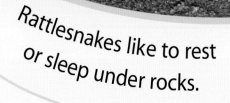

Rattlesnakes like to rest or sleep under rocks.

Pet snakes need sleep and somewhere to rest, just like in the wild. Good places for your snake to sleep include a hollow tree branch or upside-down flowerpot. You can also buy specially made nest boxes.

If your snake would naturally hibernate in the wild, you should let it hibernate for a few weeks every year. Cool the snake's **vivarium** down and give it somewhere to sleep. Ask an expert for advice.

Pet snakes need somewhere in their vivarium where they feel safe enough to rest and sleep.

Life cycle of snakes

Snakes live for different lengths of time. Most snakes live for between 10 and 25 years. Large pythons can live for 40 years or more.

Most snakes lay eggs. Some snakes, such as pythons, **incubate** their eggs. This means the female curls around the eggs to keep them a steady temperature until they hatch.

Other snakes, like boas and anacondas, have live young, and give birth to 20 or more tiny snakes.

Most snakes lay between 4 and 12 eggs, but Burmese pythons can lay up to 100!

Garter snakes usually have between 10 and 20 babies.

Garter snakes give birth to live young. Corn snakes lay eggs. Corn snakes usually have about 6–8 eggs, but can have up to 30. That's a lot of snakes!

The length of time that a snake is pregnant varies between **species**. It is difficult to tell if your snake is pregnant. It will look a bit fatter than normal, but you may not realise at all until the snake gives birth.

Common problems

In the wild, snakes may be eaten by **predators**. These are often other snakes. People also hunt them for their skins.

New farming methods destroy snake **habitats** like **rainforests** and jungles so snakes have nowhere to live.

Madagascan tree boas are in danger of dying out in the wild.

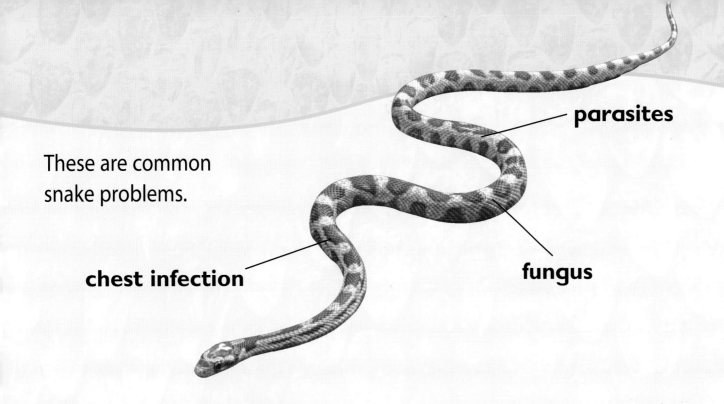

These are common snake problems.

parasites

chest infection

fungus

Itches and sneezes

Snakes can get **parasites**. These include worms and **bacteria** inside them, and fleas and mites on their skin. Your vet can give you something to treat parasites.

Snakes can get fungal infections. This is where a **fungus** grows and damages the **scales** or skin.

Snakes can get breathing problems and chest infections. These can be very serious. Always see your vet.

Now you know more about why snakes behave the way they do, you can look forward to a rewarding future with your pet.

Find out for yourself

A good owner will always want to learn more about keeping pet snakes. To find out more information about snakes, you can look in other books and on the Internet.

Books to read

Corn Snakes, R.D. Bartlett, Barron's Educational Series, 2000.
Deadly Snakes, Andrew Solway, Heinemann, 2004

Using the Internet

Explore the Internet to find out about snakes. Websites can change, so if one of the links below no longer works, don't worry. Use a search engine, such as *www.yahooligans.com* or *www.internet4kids.com*. You could try searching using the key words 'snakes' and 'pets'.

Websites

This website has lots of information about looking after pet snakes: *http://www.rspca.org.uk/servlet/Satellite?pagename=RSPCA/AnimalCare/Animals&articleid=9968279448800*

A good site for finding out more about wild snakes can be found at: *www.reptilepark.com.au*

Glossary

adapt become used to living in certain conditions

anatomy how the body is made

bacteria germs or tiny living things that can live inside other living things

breed a particular type of animal within a species

breeder someone who raises animals

captivity kept in a cage or tank rather than living in the wild

endangered in danger of dying out or being killed

food chain the links between animals that feed on each other

fungus a type of mould that can grow on a snake's skin

habitat where an animal or plant lives

incubate to keep eggs warm until they hatch

mammal an animal that has warm blood and usually fur

mate when two animals come together to make babies

parasites tiny animals that live in or on another animal and feed off it

predator animal that hunts and eats other animals

prey animals that are hunted and eaten by predators

rainforest thick forest in tropical areas of the world

reptile cold-blooded, scaly animal, like a lizard or snake

scales small hard sections that fit together to form a tough skin

sociable likes company and living in groups

species similar animals that can have babies together

tropical warm parts of the earth near the equator

venom/venomous venom is poison, and a snake that can inject venom is called venomous

vibrations tiny movements that the snake can feel in the air or through the ground

vivarium special tank designed for keeping reptiles in

Index